"Patrick Donovan has compiled an entertaining collection of common sense lessons that shed light on our day-to-day complexities."

> – James Garrettson
> *Vice President Sales, Eastern Region*
> *Qwest*

"Thought provoking…the Farmer's Almanac for daily life."

> – Joan Scully
> *Vice President Human Resources*
> *Falcon*

"A realistic view of how small things can make a big difference in our lives."

> – Dr. Ben Henry
> *Director of Training*
> *Sandals Resorts International*

TAKE CHARGE!

A Personal Guide for Taking Action

Patrick W. Donovan

Inspired Publications, Inc.

TAKE CHARGE!
A Personal Guide to Taking Action

COPYRIGHT © 1998 by Inspired Publications, Inc.
125 Delmar Street
Melbourne Beach, FL 32951

All rights reserved. No part of this work may be copied, reproduced, stored in a retrieval system, or transmitted in any form or by any means, mechanical, electronic, photocopying, audio recording, or otherwise, nor adapted to other format or application, without prior permission of the author.

ISBN 0-9664846-0-6

DEDICATION

To my late aunt, Anna Donovan. I want to thank you for being supportive in all I want to accomplish. You told me "something big" was going to happen for me. I believe because of all the support it will. You are thought of often. "All good thoughts." Thanks, Aunt Ann.

CONTENTS

Acknowledgments 8

Introduction 9

1. You Ask to Have the Power 11
2. You Put it into Perspective 17
3. You Avoid the Negative Spotlight 25
4. Hello, Are You Conscious? 31
5. You Pick Up the Pace 37
6. Your Actions Speak Louder 43
7. You Create the Conversations 51
8. You Force the Habit 59
9. You Become a Worker 65
10. You Have Luck 71
11. You Will Become It 75
12. Make Your Actions Contagious 83
13. Adopt What You Want 89

ACKNOWLEDGEMENTS

The first person I wish to acknowledge is Kerry Weismann for her numerous hours of dedication and effort toward the writing of this book. I'm sure you've seen the words to every chapter over and over in your dreams. Thanks for your hard work, encouragement and constructive feedback. Thank you, Kerry.

To all the people I've had the pleasure to live, train, talk, coach, counsel and share with over the years. Thanks to all of you.

To all the people I've trained and inspired - you've done the same for me. Thanks for all the experience.

To Eric and Krista Horning - Thanks for all the motivation!

To my parents, James and Dorothy Donovan, for instilling in my four brothers - Jim, Tim, Tom, John - and me that the only way you're going to have anything you want is by taking action.

I also know that if not for one other person this project would still be a thought rather than a reality. I'd like to thank my wife, Deon, for helping me put on paper what was in my head and for making sense of it all. Your support, encouragement, love and patience are greatly appreciated. Thanks for dusting me off. Love, Pat.

INTRODUCTION

I have always wanted to write a book. This book is an accumulated response to questions such as "Do you have a book out, Patrick?" and, "Could you please write a book as a reminder?" As well as comments including, "You should write a book, Pat," and, "You should put that in writing." It's compiled of many wise teachings, practices, observations, stories and what I've learned for myself. However, most importantly, this book is the result of taking action.

After talking about it for years now, I realized my book wasn't getting done by just talking about it. I needed to take action. Action is the key component in getting something done. When you take action, you accomplish tasks, work, goals, and dreams. You feel rewarded for your efforts.

1
YOU ASK TO HAVE THE POWER

"It's an unanswered question, but let us believe in the dignity and the importance of the question."

-Tennessee Williams

When I decided to write a book, I realized it was to help people become accomplished financially and emotionally. A person has to ask the right questions in order to achieve this type of success. Now after 17 years as a salesman, public speaker, trainer, motivator and coach, I have analyzed and recognized the power in questioning.

TAKE CHARGE!

The person who asks the right questions in a conversation has several advantages. Listed below are some examples of questions you may ask on a daily basis. This list may include questions you are typically asked by others:

- How are you?
- Where are you going?
- How much is this?
- What are you going to do?
- Are we having fun yet?

These questions are applicable to a variety of situations. The list could continue. Isn't the number of questions we ask every day astonishing? How would you feel if you realized the person asking the questions is actually in control of your conversation? Is that okay? Does it bother you or does it make you more inquisitive?

The person asking the questions is always in control. When you interview for a position

YOU ASK TO HAVE THE POWER

with a company, who initiates the questions? For example, a woman has applied for the position of customer service representative. The manager invites her to an interview. She comes into his office and he immediately slams her with questions, *"What do you know about our company? Why did you take six months off from school? Can you describe yourself in one adjective? Where do you see yourself in five years?"* The manager has authority over the situation. At the conclusion of the interview he offers the woman an opportunity to ask a question or two of her own. He still has the dominance. *"Now, do you have any questions?"* This is where the interviewee has a window of opportunity to take control. She grins and says, *"No, sir."* You know why she did not get the job offer. She needed to demonstrate her ability to steer the conversation. A customer service representative must possess a strong demeanor. A representative has to be firm and polite.

Think about children for a moment. They ask plenty of questions. Children from the age of two to four have discovered the powerful open-

TAKE CHARGE!

ended question applicable to every conversation, *"Why?"* We feel compelled, as adults, to constructively feed their curious little minds. Unfortunately, their questions might hit the point of annoyance. For example, a father and son are out walking one night. The boy asks, *"Daddy, why are the stars so bright?"* The father responds, *"I'm not sure."* Then the boy starts his tirade of *"why, why, why?"* The father takes control of the conversation, *"Why are you so interested in the stars?"* The boy squishes up his forehead in thought, *"Well, I'm five years old; that's my job."* Suddenly the boy is challenged to think, and the father has gained control. The father places his hand on his son's shoulder, *"As a 5 year old, do you want to start heading home?"*

People ask the typical questions I mentioned earlier but they want descriptive answers. They need to ask the right questions. The best question to ask is *"Why?"* because that compels people to answer fully. To obtain the information you need to know, it's imperative that you use the right format for gaining detail and getting people to elaborate.

 **YOU ASK TO HAVE THE POWER**

Don't forget! Whenever you need to stimulate conversation or open the lines of communication, ask - don't tell. The person asking the questions is in control.

2

YOU PUT IT INTO PERSPECTIVE

> "Rule #1: Don't sweat the small stuff.
>
> Rule #2: It's all small stuff."
>
> *-Dr. Michael Mantell*

One person's problem may be another person's opportunity. It all depends on how you view the situation. If you keep things in proper perspective you will maintain the advantage of noticing the opportunity rather than constantly being forced to view the problem. I have learned to listen, sit back, and observe situations rather than simply react in haste.

TAKE CHARGE!

Think for a moment on how essential it is to put aspects of your life into proper perspective. Your personal life, your work, the way you interact with a stranger on the street, or behind a slow car, your perspective on the situation determines your reaction.

It's like the old story of the husband who came home to find a note on his kitchen counter, *"Dear Ralph,"* it began, *"Don't bother looking in the refrigerator, it's empty. I also cleaned out the bank account. You might notice the other car is missing. Don't worry about your daughter in college; she's expecting but all the guys said they'll chip in and help out. I'm leaving. Good-bye. Alice."* Ralph blinked several times in mortification and continued to read, *"P.S. Just Kidding, I forgot to pick up your shirts at the dry cleaner's. I just thought we should put it in proper perspective."*

If Alice had not put the trivial matter that she forgot to pick up Ralph's shirts into proper perspective, his response may have been irate. If her letter had only stated, *"I'm so sorry I forgot to pick up your shirts. Please don't be mad at*

YOU PUT IT INTO PERSPECTIVE

me," Ralph would have said, *"What? Now what am I going to wear to work tomorrow?"*

Another example of putting things into proper perspective is present in our every day lives. Have you ever hit a wall and said, *"I'm just doing this task the same old way?"* You need more options. You need to take a fresh look at the way you are doing your every day tasks, even if your methodology is already effective. When something goes wrong, try to find and highlight the advantages.

For instance, a reservations supervisor working for a major air carrier found out that his employer had decided to no longer use the small airport he was based out of for the past sixteen years. The airline gave him two startling options: (1) Move his entire family across the country, or (2) Start part-time at the closest international airport even though it would mean a demotion. The man chose the latter, even though it meant not having the same status. Most people would have been furious in his situation; however, he diverted his focus to

TAKE CHARGE!

the positives. At least he had a job doing something he enjoyed. He didn't have to move his family. He could still commute daily to and from work. He found a way to make the change good and positive.

Proper perspective can be applicable to several areas. You may have seen the athlete who scores a touchdown then spikes the ball or shakes a little groove. Or the one who scores a basket and waves his hands in the air as if to say *"Look at me!"*. But what do some of the greatest athletes of all time do?

Barry Sanders scores a touchdown and hands the football back to the referee. Michael Jordan hits a jump shot and hustles to the other end of the court to play defense. They do not perform a full minute circus show. Both athletes act like they are going to be there again. They want their fans to know this performance is not a rare occurrence. They keep it in the proper perspective.

Think about the last time you were really disturbed by something you could not control.

YOU PUT IT INTO PERSPECTIVE

Perhaps someone crashed into your car, or maybe you lost your favorite watch. Now contemplate how a constructive reaction can make all the difference. For example, in the first case, at least no one was hurt in the accident. In the latter case, as frustrating as it may seem, the watch was only materialistic. You can buy another watch. Put yourself in a good mood when you come home from work, school or errands. Focus on enjoying life instead of concentrating on all the work you have left to do.

Your proper perspective will create your positive attitude.

Don't forget! No matter what the situation, before you react, take charge and put it into proper perspective.

"Perspective is worth 80 I.Q. points."
-Alan Kay

3

YOU AVOID THE NEGATIVE SPOTLIGHT

> "Most of the trouble in the world is caused by people wanting to be important."
>
> - *T.S. Eliot*

As a child, my friends and I used to play a game called flashlight tag. The game was very similar to hide and seek but was always played at night or in darkness. While playing flashlight tag, we had to hide from a person who hunted for us and then tried to flash the beam of light on us. The goal was to avoid the beam of the light and get home safe. In other words, avoid that negative spotlight!

TAKE CHARGE!

On the night of a movie premier, some of us are delighted to witness our favorite actors and actresses walk the rich, red carpet path in the warm glow of a Hollywood spotlight. On the other hand, you know a harsh spotlight is used by the police in a helicopter pursuit or to locate an escaped convict from prison. In the first case, the celebrities absorb the spotlight and welcome it. The glow of the spotlight may help further their careers. As movie stars, they have prepared ways to effectively utilize their presence in it. In the latter case, the convict flees from the spotlight. The spotlight could prevent his escape and locate where he is hiding. These are two extremes of the spotlight effect.

Most of us only see the positive side of the spotlight effect. We welcome recognition when we do something well at work, at home, or in the community. However, think of the repercussions a negative spotlight may spread. If you neglect to give a credit check to a potential client, accidentally leave the milk on the counter so it spoils, or forget to show up for

YOU AVOID THE NEGATIVE SPOTLIGHT

your shift at the firehouse's fun fair, you would rather people didn't notice. You want to be ignored if you are not living up to your end of the contract. Which beam would you prefer?

Some people get caught in the negative spotlight by not performing as they said they would during the hiring process with a company. Others promise people, such as family members, co-workers, and neighbors that they will do something, and then they do not show up. Another group of people are the ones that say *"No problem. I can do that for you,"* or *"Sure, I'll get that done tomorrow."* But this group finds that there is so much they have taken on that they can't possibly accomplish everything. If you choose to be in the spotlight, make sure if you *"talk the talk"*, you can *"walk the walk"*. Do not generate hype for your performance unless you plan on following through accordingly.

The key is to manipulate the positive spotlight effect. When you get recognition for a job well done, never take all of the credit. Bring atten-

TAKE CHARGE!

tion to the members of your committee or team, give gratitude to your managers, friends, and relatives for their support and guidance. They helped you make it happen. If you truly believe that you completed the task entirely on your own, stop and think about the extra hours you worked and your significant other did not complain or the education your parents funded. Focus your thoughts on the professor that motivated you to think critically or the coffee shop that let you linger a half an hour after they closed so you could complete a project.

If you have found you are in the negative spotlight when you ultimately would prefer not to be, identify the main reason you are there. Perhaps you have drawn away from supportive people and have put yourself out in your office as independent rather than interdependent. Or you may have excelled at something until your tasks have become standardized and you are bored. Decide what steps can be taken to change and give yourself a measurable length of time to accomplish these steps. You have to deliver what you promise, challenge yourself,

YOU AVOID THE NEGATIVE SPOTLIGHT

and acknowledge the support of others.

Don't forget! You have a choice of which spotlight you want to be viewed under and you alone can control this.

4

HELLO, ARE YOU CONSCIOUS?

"The best way to make your dreams come true is to wake up."

-*Paul Valery*

"It's a left hook to the jaw and he's down! Oh wait... He's up! He's up on his feet very quickly but the referee stops the fight. He's out on his feet! Even though his eyes are open, he has no idea where he is."

The boxer in this scenario is conscious; however, right now you would have to remind him of that. You do not need to be a boxer to experience this feeling. There are periods of time in our lives that slip by us unconsciously every day.

TAKE CHARGE!

Take responsibility for your actions. Be conscious, please! There are several unconscious people walking around on this Earth with their eyes open. You may believe these people are inconsiderate, however, they are not. If a person is inconsiderate, they have made a voluntary decision to not care. It's not that unconscious people don't care, it's that they're oblivious to their surroundings and aren't aware of their actions or the repercussions from their lack of actions.

An unconscious person gets in the way of a conscious person on an everyday basis. The unconscious person walks aimlessly around airports, drives through traffic at 40 miles per hour sight-seeing when the speed limit is 55 mph, and looks right past her manager's ear when he is telling her what she needs to do on Tuesday. You will find an unconscious person utilizing one phrase twenty times a day, *"Oh, excuse me."*

For instance, you may only have twenty minutes left on your lunch hour due to heavy traffic, and the fast food line of nine people has

HELLO, ARE YOU CONSCIOUS?

dwindled down to one person ahead of you. Before you even have a chance to look at your watch and sigh with relief, the person in front of you mumbles, *"Let me see...do you sell cheeseburgers here? What does that come with, some ketchup? I don't like ketchup, can you hold that? On second thought, do you sell milkshakes? What flavors? Can I get a taste of..."* Instinctively, you might want to kick the person in the rear. If you knew he had not seen the large menu with photographs that even a five year old child could understand, you would have pointed it out to him eight people ago. The unmindful man continues, *"On second thought, what do you like? Is there a guarantee on that?"* You are already in another line before he starts counting four dollars worth of pennies and nickels or attempts to write a check.

How can you become more conscious? First you need to prioritize. Make it a priority to know what is going on in your job, your life, as well as your everyday functions. Be conscious, be purposeful, and be the best. Consciously think about how your actions (or lack of ac-

TAKE CHARGE!

tion) affect your friends, co-workers, and family.

At the workplace you have seen co-workers that do not prepare properly to deal with the public. Unfortunately, due to unconscious habits, these people do not change their mood or get everything in place before they begin their day. A conscious effort makes the difference between success and dismal failure. Observe the things going on around you and look for ways to better communicate. Think before you get behind the wheel of your car. Think of how your actions may be affecting others right now. Think of several options and choose the best one, not just the first one that comes to mind. Be conscious about the job you have accepted and what you are doing. You may be receiving calls from potential customers, analyzing the monthly expense reports, or filing patients insurance claims. Be conscious of the people that surround you. They may have a tighter schedule than you or are experiencing problems which affect their behavior.

HELLO, ARE YOU CONSCIOUS?

Be conscious of what obstacles prevent you from accomplishing what you need to. Keep an open mind about change. Take excellent notes with clients and participate in discussions. Ask your customer what she wants. Notice what motivates your children to clean their rooms and do their homework.

Ask yourself four questions:

1. What am I doing right now?

_____

2. How are my actions affecting others?

_____

3. Am I using my time effectively?

_____

4. Is there something I should be doing that I am not?

_____

If yes, what?

_____

TAKE CHARGE!

If you have found that some of your actions are indeed unconscious, the next step after acknowledgment is change. You are now taking proactive action. You have already become conscious.

Don't forget! Conscious people think before they go about their everyday lives. They plan, strategize and pay attention to their surroundings. Become more conscious.

5

YOU PICK UP THE PACE

> "Once you say you're going to settle for second, that's what happens to you in life, I find."
>
> -*John F. Kennedy*

It is 5:00 p.m, you just arrived at the airport for a 5:30 p.m. departure to the vacation spot of a lifetime. If you miss this flight, you will need to catch the next flight which is not available until the next morning. Rather than give up and go look for a hotel room near the airport, you decide you can make this flight if you maneuver quickly.

Running through the airport, dodging baby carriages, business travelers, and the rest of the crowd, you reach your gate with two minutes to spare. Later that evening, as you sit on the

TAKE CHARGE!

beach viewing the spectacular Caribbean Sea, you and your companion agree it was worth the rush to make your flight.

YOU PICK UP THE PACE

In order to achieve, you need to pick up the pace. When you were young and you wanted to keep up with the older kids on the block, you had to learn to pedal your bicycle faster and pick up the pace to hang out. If you wanted good grades in school, or to play varsity sports before you were a senior, you had to pick up the pace. To excel as a worker at your company by practicing, educating yourself, listening and retaining information, and meeting difficult deadlines, you had to pick up the pace.

If you are living in a world of *"It didn't used to work that way,"* or *"I don't like change, things are moving too fast for me to keep up,"* you have to pick up the pace. You need to react, not ignore. Change is inevitable in business with new technologies and new markets. The amount of change is overwhelming, as in the overnight success of information technology companies. In order to keep up with change, you need to increase your pace.

A good example of picking up the pace is shown

TAKE CHARGE!

in the case of the manufacturers of the Saturn car. In the early years of production, the car proved so popular that the Saturn people couldn't keep up with the demand. In response to that, management was forced to build a new plant and add to the production schedule. They recognized immediately that they needed to pick up the pace.

With regard to those in the field of sales, forget about a forty-hour work week! You will need to go in early and stay late to be competitive. You'll also find it necessary to study more, really know your product and understand the psychology of your buyers. You need to pick up the pace to be productive.

Don't forget! In order to stand out from the rest, you need to pick up the pace and set a standard of your own that others will strive to emulate. If you would like to be a leader, do not just pick up the pace, set the pace.

"Even if you're on the right track, you'll get run over if you just sit there."

—*Will Rogers*

6

YOUR ACTIONS SPEAK LOUDER

> "The common conception is that motivation leads to action, but the reverse is true…action precedes motivation."
>
> *-Robert McKain*

Talk, talk, talk, talk, and talk! I know I have done my share of it. Ironically, I have noticed that until I did something about initiating action on those words, all those words were just plain talk. I always talked about what I was going to do with my life. I was going here,

TAKE CHARGE!

going to do this and going to do that. However, nothing was going to happen until I got up and actually did it.

Now I do not talk as much about what I plan on doing, and where I plan on traveling. Instead I find myself talking about what I have already done and where I have already been.

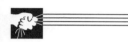

YOUR ACTIONS SPEAK LOUDER

There are multiple things in this world that we see everyday that are the result of someone taking action. Think for a moment of something you have seen, either at a discount store or on cable television, that you had previously recognized a need for and even contemplated creating. Your mind became overwhelmed with, *"Hey, I thought of that first!"* With seven billion people on this planet, you were not alone. But the other person who has his patent on your mutual idea is absorbing the benefits because he has taken action.

A wise person once commented that before a child reaches the age of ten, she has had at least one idea that would have made her financially secure for the endurance of her lifetime. The child, usually unsure of how to take action and monetarily short, did nothing with the idea.

Think for a moment about the selected few that proceeded with their ideas and are now financially set for their existence. That Slinky, Hoola-hoop, safety pin, paper clip, and wind

TAKE CHARGE!

shield wiper are simple, common items. The volume sold year in and year out is astonishing. Any of these items could have been your product and your profit.

Back in 1980, I met a man from Boca Raton, Florida who was a sound man at a nightclub. One evening a stranger came into his club and bought a round of drinks for everyone. The sound man explained: *"Toward the end of the night, the stranger bought the place another round of drinks and as if that was not enough, the stranger then invited everyone to his place after the bar closed."* The sound man continued, *"At his house, the stranger had a bar even bigger than the one at the club. I was anxious to find out what this man did for a living, so I asked him when I got a moment. I discovered that the stranger was already retired."*

My friend eventually learned that years earlier the stranger had purchased greasy fast food french fries that leaked through the thin paper container onto his car seat. He recognized the need for an effective and durable container for

 **YOUR ACTIONS SPEAK LOUDER**

french fries. So now, when you eat french fries from the cardboard box that most fast food chains utilize today, think about how this stranger receives a percentage of the profits for each container sold. He attributes his success to the action he took.

Taking action is also important with regard to talking about doing something as opposed to actually doing it. Consider the number of hotels that claim to have impeccable customer service. These claims are plastered all over their marketing materials, on little cards in the bathrooms, and on business cards. These words have no credibility when the phone rings for five minutes if you call the lobby for extra towels, or if the hotel neglects to give you your requested wake up call. These are not the actions of a hotel that has notable customer service. Now consider the hotel that takes the necessary action to make you a satisfied customer. You are picked up from the airport on time, you're greeted at the door, the room you want is ready, and you are offered a complete, complementary breakfast. In addition to a se-

TAKE CHARGE!

curity guard, you will find an ATM, shoe shine, newspaper, extra towels, and all the other things to ensure your stay is comfortable. You come to the conclusion that when there is good customer service, you do not have to be told. Their actions do the talking.

There are also those people who aspire to have a better occupation. They give excuses for not taking charge. They point out the obvious, *"Well, if she didn't have that degree,"* and *"If he didn't get that lucky job as production assistant out of college."* People that take action to advance and get to a level of excellence at their occupation are the ones who are most rewarded. There are more people that possess the ability to do things than those who are actually doing them. The qualifier is the people who do them, want them. Take pride in your actions.

YOUR ACTIONS SPEAK LOUDER

List below five things you would love to have or you would love to do.

1. _____
2. _____
3. _____
4. _____
5. _____

Now list what it would take for you to achieve each item.

1. _____
2. _____
3. _____
4. _____
5. _____

TAKE CHARGE!

List the time and date you will begin working on each item.

1. _____

2. _____

3. _____

4. _____

5. _____

Get up in the middle of the night to write those ideas down. Keep a journal, book, cassette recorder or even a "post it" available for a collection of good ideas. Take action on those ideas.

Don't forget! If you want something enough, you can have it but you need to take action.

7
YOU CREATE THE CONVERSATIONS

"Half the world is composed of people who have something to say and can't and the other half who have nothing to say and keep on saying it."

-*Robert Frost*

As I was reading through some evaluations for a recent seminar I facilitated for LCI International, I noticed one attendee after the other had written in the comment section: *"I learned so much about why having conversations with our clients is so important."* In addition, one person wrote, *"You're right! I have conversations with my family and friends. Why do I get so serious and stuffy with my clients? I'm actually interrogating them instead of conversing with them!"* I had no

TAKE CHARGE!

idea the impact our discussion on creating conversations had on this group until I reviewed the evaluations.

I then remembered one of the key things this group hoped to gain from the seminar and that was to be better able to help their clients. The best way to help someone is to know what they need. The only way to know what they need is to have a conversation with them.

# YOU CREATE THE CONVERSATIONS

I believe conversations educate all of us. We simply learn that "my way" isn't necessarily the "only way". As a public speaker, I have addressed thousands of people through corporate training seminars and inspirational presentations. I have completed thousands of hours of one-on-one coaching sessions with upper, middle and lower management in addition to salespeople, customer service representatives, and administrators. I have found that successful people possess one asset that stands out from the not-so-great: fantastic communication skills. Most importantly, these people have conversations, not interrogations with their friends, co-workers, and clients.

The most successful people ask challenging questions or give firm statements to get others to talk. They have a great knack for listening to others rather than just hearing the words that are spoken to them. Their communication skills are polished as well as effective. As discussed in Chapter One, you can control your conversations by taking charge and asking the right questions. The ability to

TAKE CHARGE!

communicate effectively is utilizing this power to a higher degree.

You have seen famous interviewers on television. The noteworthy ones are brilliant at generating conversations with their guests. The guest may be anyone from a political leader to a soap opera heart throb. These interviewers usually begin with a statement rather than a question, and they say it with confidence and control.

The interview begins with a phrase such as, *"Please tell me what it was like..."* or *"Explain to me how you felt when..."*. Professionals, including those in management, sales, customer service, counseling, etc. also demonstrate this method of getting a conversation going. Even parents exhibit conversation stimulation successfully by using this format of *"Explain to me," "Please tell me,"* and *"Talk to me about it."* These steering statements require a response of three or more words which is what you need to have a conversation.

The other part of communication is listening.

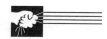 **YOU CREATE THE CONVERSATIONS**

Instead of responding with another predetermined question, good interviewers ask the next question based on their guest's prior answers. These interviewers convince their guest of their listening skills with the animation of body language including head nods, encouraging smiles, and other facial and hand expressions. In addition, the interviewers verbally acknowledge the key points of the conversation. The gestures come naturally to us in comfortable situations with our family and friends. However, in the corporate world, we have a tendency to become too structured or serious. As if reading from a script, we interrogate our clients and customers instead of conversing with them. Sometimes, we unconsciously have the same problem with our families and friends. Common knowledge holds that the fundamental questions we should ask are: who, when, what, where, and how. We were taught to position these words at the beginning of a question. However, if you want someone to elaborate for you, is this a good way to get them to talk? These questions only require the person to re-

TAKE CHARGE!

ply in three words or less. Therefore, the person asking the questions is not generating conversation.

Another way to understand interrogating questions is to consider the way a detective or law enforcement official would gather facts and evidence for an investigation:

> *"What's your full name?"*
>
> *"Where were you on the night of...?"*
>
> *"Who else was with you?"*
>
> *"What were you doing there?"*
>
> *"When did you leave?"*

Again, these questions only result in short answers.

The examples below show you what to ask or say to stimulate conversation:

> *"Please describe for me how I can help you."*
>
> *"Explain to me what is going on in here."*
>
> *"Tell me how you would like this to look."*

 **YOU CREATE THE CONVERSATIONS**

"Why does it bother you?"

"Outline our options for this project."

Questions that result in short answers do not have to be entirely avoided; however, your best bet is to only use them in appropriate situations. Whether you interrogate or converse can be determined by qualifying the information you want to gather from clients, friends, or co-workers. Interrogating is an excellent way to ensure accurate details but exercise caution. People do not like to put on the spot nor do they prefer this type of questioning. Most importantly, listen to what others are saying.

Don't forget! Create conversation by using strong questions or statements. Listen to the response before you ask the next question. Always let them know you're listening.

8
YOU FORCE THE HABIT

"If it is to be, it is up to me."

-William H. Johnson

For a period of time in my life, I found myself losing focus whenever I sat down to read a book. I would start to read a chapter only to find myself drifting off into a daydream. All of a sudden I had to start over to comprehend what I had just read. Then I discovered the reason for this. I was not reading enough material on a regular basis. I had gotten out of the habit. Instead, I was watching more television or doing other things for recreation. Unfortunately, I felt like I was losing some creativity.

I decided the only way I could get back that missing creativity was to retrain myself. So I began to read more, forcing myself daily to pick

TAKE CHARGE!

up the newspaper, grab a magazine or a book. Now I am back to daily reading. I have learned to force the habit and save the daydreaming for later.

YOU FORCE THE HABIT

You most likely have a habitual inclination, perhaps even several. Do you find yourself explaining certain behaviors due to force of habit? Force *of* habit is the result of repetition to point that you can do an act without cognition. You can learn to do an activity by repetition, like when you were taught how to ride a bicycle or drive a standard shift automobile.

An example of force of habit is a father that wakes up without an alarm at 4:30 every morning even though he retired twenty years ago. Or the lady on the way to a dentist appointment who absentmindedly turns left as though she were going to work when she really wanted to turn right.

In order to force *the* habit, you have to claim these actions and make concrete efforts to overcome them. You need to create your own "habitude" - a combination of habit + attitude.

Maybe you have wanted to lose a few extra pounds but feel like you're fighting a losing battle. Examine your routine. Instead of mak-

TAKE CHARGE!

ing that cup of coffee after dinner which tastes even better with your usual two or three cookies, get up and go for a walk. Break the habit of coffee and instill the habitude of walking.

Or perhaps you wish to spend more quality time with your children. Instead of giving in to your habit of turning on the television each night, create a new habitude of reading with your children or share a mutual hobby.

The first step to forcing the habit is to make a list of things you wish you were able to do. Perhaps you would like to sculpt your body or excel at a sport. You may aspire to be promoted at work, to earn a special degree or to own a business. You can create habitude by empowering it.

YOU FORCE THE HABIT

Try the following exercise:

List some items you would like to accomplish:

_____

_____

_____

_____

_____

What are you doing now to accomplish these?

_____

_____

_____

_____

_____

What steps should you be taking to accomplish these items?

_____

_____

_____

_____

_____

TAKE CHARGE!

Forcing the habit can improve the quality of the time you spend at work, with family and friends, and with yourself. Force the habit if you want to change. Do not permit force of habit to command your life.

Don't forget! If you're tired of the same old thing day-in and day-out, you can change it by forcing the habit. Develop a new habitude!

9

YOU BECOME A WORKER

"Go out with a definite purpose and stay with your work as long as that purpose remains definite."

-Bobby Jones

No one wants to get up and go to a job they dislike. Unfortunately, not everyone has a choice of whether or not they can quit that job. As a result, what are the options? Oh yeah, you can go through the motions or call in sick occasionally to job hunt. However, when it comes down to it, you are still there.

What I found had worked for me, instead of ignoring it and disliking it, was performing the best I could at that job. I challenged and bet myself that if I worked diligently to exceed the

TAKE CHARGE!

company's expectations of me in that position, and I still disliked it, I would leave. I would not permit myself to find a new employer until I tried working harder and smarter for a set period of time.

We usually dislike anything if we just go through the motions. Housework, homework, relationships, marriages, the category does not matter. When you decide to succeed at something, you take on a whole new attitude and things begin to happen in your favor.

YOU BECOME A WORKER

There are those of us who are workers, and there are those of us who are work-fors. Workers and work-fors can be found in every office and in every occupation.

Workers are the people who are committed to making it happen. They are continually fine-tuning and elevating tasks to the next level. They understand why they accepted a position and what it is they can bring on board to make a positive impact at their job, home, or wherever they spend time. Workers know what motivates them to drive forward at all times. You will notice workers rapidly getting promotions, offering assistance, creating solutions, and accomplishing twenty hours of work in a ten hour work day. Workers pre-plan their weekends and days off, getting up early to fit in a game of touch football, furniture shopping, washing the car, in addition to dinner with their friends.

There are also work-fors. Work-fors are those people who just go to a job or just collect a paycheck. Work-fors are extremely

TAKE CHARGE!

different from workers because they tend to do just what it takes– no more and no less. You will recognize work-fors glancing at their watch, getting to the office at exactly 9:01 a.m. and leaving at precisely 4:59 p.m. Their lunch break is always one hour, even if they are on a deadline.

At home, work-fors only do the dishes on "their night" and ask friends to pick up a couple of items at the grocery store for them, so they do not have to go themselves. They only offer to help at the elementary school when it is mandatory. Work-fors tend to accept where they are. They divert from change. Workers, on the other hand, are committed to ongoing education, updating technology in their industry, reading trade magazines, attending seminars, and learning about updated products and services.

One group is not smarter or better than the other. The workers are simply dedicated and committed to moving everything up a notch.

If you are a manager, you can steer an employee

 **YOU BECOME A WORKER**

onto the path of becoming a worker. You can paint the picture with the following methodology:

- Outline what you and the employee agreed upon when you hired him. Tell him what he has contributed to the company so far.

- Ask the employee what he would do if he owned the company. Ask him how he would run it and what qualities he would look for when interviewing potential employees.

- Have the employee compare what he has said to how he actually performs. Lead him to the realization that he has to practice what he preaches.

In order for you to transform a work-for into a worker, you have to be a worker yourself. Make sure as a manager, you have these practices of a worker imbedded into your everyday processes.

Identify where you are with your life and career. List the beneficial traits you possess. To

TAKE CHARGE!

become a worker, determine how many of these traits you can raise to the next level by furthering your education or by making a little, positive change to the way you are currently performing? Only you can decide whether you want to be a worker or a work-for.

Don't forget! Workers fine tune all aspects of their life ongoing. Work-fors just go through the motions. Be a worker.

10
YOU HAVE LUCK

> "I am a great believer in luck, and I find the harder I work, the more luck I have."
>
> *-Thomas Jefferson*

There is nothing greater than the realization of how lucky you can be if you organize and take action in your life, instead of rolling the dice and waiting to see what happens.

TAKE CHARGE!

There's a group of people in society we label the lucky ones. This group scores luck on a frequent basis. They always get the vacant parking spaces close to the entrance at the airport, office building, shopping mall, or wherever they may happen to drive. These people should actually be labeled the persistent ones. They control the factors they can in order to prosper with good fortune and success.

The lucky parking space locators pull into a lot and concentrate on what they're doing. By starting close to the building, they quickly notice people walking out to their cars and stalk, well not actually stalk, but follow them. They are alert to their surroundings. The unlucky parking space locators accelerate to the only empty one in the back of the lot, 3.2 miles from the building. They later complain when they get caught in the afternoon rainstorm (especially if they left the top down on the car!) and decide they have bad luck. Is it a luck factor or an action factor?

YOU HAVE LUCK

I have a friend in Ireland who views the luck factor rather logically. He says when he makes a decision in life, it is like catching a train. First, he decides what his destination is. Next, he purchases a ticket and waits for the train. Finally, when the train arrives, he determines whether to board the train or not. Whatever happens is not based on luck, but the action he takes to board the train.

Luck does not correlate with success as much as we suspect. People who take action create their own fortune rather than relying on luck. People who have luck with money and investments are conscious of the market. They research their options and enact careful investments. People who possess luck in the work force understand the ratio of odds. They do not sit at their sloppy desk and wait for the sale to magically appear. On the contrary, they take action to generate the business: More marketing + more qualified calls = more $$$.

If you are lucky, or you know someone who you consider to be lucky, do the following exercise:

TAKE CHARGE!

I believe I am lucky or that someone else is lucky because I/they:

_____

_____

_____

After you have made your list, take a closer look at the reasons why you or this acquaintance is lucky. Is it because your mom is Irish and you wear green underwear on St. Patrick's Day? Is it because your friend wears the same socks every day of his rookie season? I doubt it.

Now list what actions have been taken by you or someone else to create this luck:

1) _____

2) _____

3) _____

4) _____

Don't forget! If you want to find a rare novel, you can wait and hope it magically appears, or you can take action and call around to get a copy. *You* decide if you are a lucky one.

11

YOU WILL BECOME IT

> "If you can believe it, you can achieve it. If you can dream it, you can become it."
>
> -W.A. Ward

My wife and I wanted a pond in the backyard. We yearned to settle back in patio furniture and watch the fish swim and enjoy the water lilies stretching out of the water towards the Florida sunshine. We began reading "how to" books discussing aquatic ponds, plants, and varieties of fish. As you could only expect, a section of our yard blossomed into our exact vision. We did it ourselves, by taking charge, and now we are enjoying the fruits of our education and labor.

TAKE CHARGE!

I recently saw a news program that talked about a teacher who started an educational program for 39 children with learning disabilities. The first thing she gave them was a mission statement: "Your I WILL is more important than your IQ.!". She then went on to also teach them about Shakespeare, math and other academic subjects. The results were more than commendable: 32 of those students graduated from college. Some received doctorates, others earned masters and higher-learning degrees. Those that did not graduate from college succeeded in owning and operating profitable businesses. Zero ended up dead. Zero ended up teenage parents. Zero were in drug rehabilitation. All thirty-nine were successful. When asked to recall what they could attribute their prosperity to, the students did not say Shakespeare. They all directed their gratitude towards the teacher who sheltered them with love and emphasis on education. Most of all, each of the students encountered each day with the knowledge acquired from their teacher that **"I WILL was more important than IQ."**

YOU WILL BECOME IT

You can not blame education. However, you can blame your lack of education. If your will to learn is strong enough, there is a way to do it. Education does not necessarily mean a formal education. Read every book, magazine, and newspaper you can. Expand your cognition. Automobiles, cooking, fashion, and politics are areas that may be of interest. Learn a new language, master the art of photography, analyze the stock market, memorize Greek mythology.

If you continually find yourself thinking that you are not paid enough for what you are worth as an employee, ask yourself why you are still at that job. Is it because your job is convenient and you don't have too much to worry about? Or maybe you don't feel like learning something new.

Try the following exercise to set yourself on a new path:

Finish each phrase with an aspiration of your own:

1)   If I could go back to school without any

TAKE CHARGE!

limitations on how much I could spend, I would study _____.

2) If a publisher approached me and told me that he would publish any book I wrote, it would be about _____.

3) If I could live in one country for a year to learn everything about the culture, I would choose the country of _____ because _____.

4) If the government gave me one billion dollars and instructed me to allocate it to any philanthropy I wished, I would start with _____.

Do not be afraid to dream and do not be afraid to live that dream. You might be doing fine right now with your high school and/or your college education, your vocational school and perhaps a little grad school on the side but could you be doing even more? Take advantage of seminars offered by your employer. Put a little twist on your wisdom to enhance it. Bring it to another level. One key to success is to re-

YOU WILL BECOME IT

member that education is a constant process.

Don't forget! If you want something, you can go get it and no one can stop you. It takes goal setting, planning, determination and taking action. If you live it, you can become it.

"We are what we pretend to be, so we must be careful about what we pretend to be."
–*Kurt Vonnegut*

12
MAKE YOUR ACTIONS CONTAGIOUS

> "The only good advice is a good example. You don't tell them a whole lot of anything. You show them by doing."
>
> *-Ossie Davis*

My parents were probably the best example of what it takes to make it in this world. I do not mean that from a financial stand point alone. When they were raising my brothers and me, they constantly demonstrated to us how to treat others, enjoy life, not take things for granted, and provide help and encouragement for those who were less fortunate than ourselves. I hope

TAKE CHARGE!

I am passing these positive traits down to others I have encountered in my life. Thanks, Mom & Dad!

MAKE YOUR ACTIONS CONTAGIOUS

If you take positive actions for yourself and build your esteem, you have an effect on others that is immeasurable. You can inspire people in many ways. Your actions and personality become contagious.

For example, my friend related to me the story of a guy driving on the state turnpike, stopping at every toll booth and dutifully depositing his money. As he was paying the attendant at the last booth, he handed her a five dollar bill and said: *"This is for me and the four cars behind me."* As my friend was one of the four drivers, she was pleasantly surprised to find her toll had already been paid. Because of this unknown man's example of generosity, my friend repeated the gesture when she was traveling on the turnpike again that month. It's very probable that one of the other travelers affected by the man's generosity also did the same.

At work, a contagious attitude can lead to remarkable success and recognition. It is important for managers to inspire rather than influence. You have to train the trainer to inspire

TAKE CHARGE!

others to perform at the highest level rather than train the trainer as only a teacher.

Make yourself contagious in a favorable way. We should welcome an outbreak of inspiration or an epidemic of good will. Our goal should be to infect everyone. Write down some bullet points to identify and constantly improve the qualities you would like to spread:

_____

_____

_____

_____

_____

Repeat daily.

If you have a successful and productive lifestyle, inspire others. Share your secrets. Remember when you mastered multiplication tables? You were so excited because you got the orange dinosaur stamp by your name on the wall. Remember the satisfaction you felt after you helped your friend earn them? Your multipli-

MAKE YOUR ACTIONS CONTAGIOUS

cation performance was even better after you shared your secret, and you helped someone else attain his goals.

Life is difficult at times. We need all the help we can get. Take help, offer help, and give help.

Don't forget! Whatever you do, people see it, hear it and sometimes feel it. So make sure your actions are positive because they affect more than just yourself.

13
ADOPT WHAT YOU WANT

"Run around with decent folk, and your own decent instincts will be strengthened."

- Stanley Walker

Just think what you would be like if you could wave a magic wand and possess all the inner traits of people you admire. What is it you would wish for? Is it self-esteem, friendliness, honesty, integrity, ability to perform at a different level? Guess what? You are holding the magic wand right now. Stop wishing and start doing. From this day forward you choose what it is you want. No one else has as much control over you as you. Go for it. Enjoy it. Become it.

TAKE CHARGE!

When you were a teenager, you wanted to be a superstar. You had aspirations to become a writer, an athlete, a musician, a dancer, an actress, a model, or a politician. As an adolescent, you may have devoured fashion magazines and emulated models by practicing their makeup techniques or copying their fashion accessories. Or sports magazines may have been your choice along with practicing those tricky shots you saw star athletes perform. Sometimes as we mature, we forget how valuable it is to learn from others and develop positive attributes from role models.

You already know that very nice person. Whenever you talk about this person, you say, *"Boy, that guy couldn't have an enemy in the world,"* or, *"That woman is so sharp. Her life has just got to be really clicking."* Do you want those qualities? Go get them. Wait, here come your excuses... *"Oh, yeah, well they have money,"* and *"Her life is perfect. I'd be that nice if I had everything going for me."* Rather than making excuses for why you can not be like these people, make up your mind that you can and adopt the traits

 **ADOPT WHAT YOU WANT**

that make those people so special.

One Virginia college student drove cross country with a friend of hers that was moving to San Diego. They were forced to spend up to fourteen hours a day traveling in a cramped two-door car. After helping her friend settle in, the student returned home and tried to pinpoint how she had spent every minute of eighteen days with the same person and never once got irritated. Even with little sleep, little food, and barely any money, she had a wonderful experience. She realized it was because of her friend's attitude. Her friend always pointed out the bright side of the situation. So the student decided to try doing this in her own life. All of a sudden, going to classes and walking two miles from the commuter lot became fun. She imitated the positive attitude of her friend and effectively adopted this attribute to improve her personality. She even caught herself contemplating, *"What would my friend do in this situation?"* The action of adoption has a pyramid effect with one action building upon another.

TAKE CHARGE!

Brainstorm on the traits of people you really enjoy spending time with. Write down five of these traits:

_____

_____

_____

_____

_____

Why are these traits important to you? Why do you like them so much? Why have you noticed them? Analyze these attributes. You might find words like "trustworthy" and "honest" on your list. Other notable characteristics you might have listed include "loving, caring, empathic, humorous, and sympathetic." Do you believe that others see these qualities in your personality? Would you like others to find these qualities in your personality? Once you acknowledge the favorable characteristics of the people around you, emulate them in your own life.

ADOPT WHAT YOU WANT

Don't forget! Live your life based on what you admire in yourself and others. Adopt what you want.

ORDER FORM

Take Charge!
A Personal Guide for Taking Action

1–99 copies _____copies @ $11.95 each
100–250 copies _____copies @ $10.95 each
251+ copies _____copies @ $9.95 each

To place an order, call toll-free (800)531-0707 or order by mail using this form. Orders may be faxed to (407)728-2977.

Name _____
Job title _____
Organization _____
Phone _____
Address _____
P.O.Box _____
City _____ State _____ Zip _____
Country _____
Purchase order # (if applicable) _____

Applicable sales tax, shipping and handling charge will be added. Price subject to change.

☐ Check enclosed

☐ Money order enclosed

☐ Please invoice (Minimum order $100. Orders of less than $100 require pre-payment)

or mail order directly to:
Inspired Publications, Inc.
125 Delmar Street
Melbourne Beach, Florida 32951